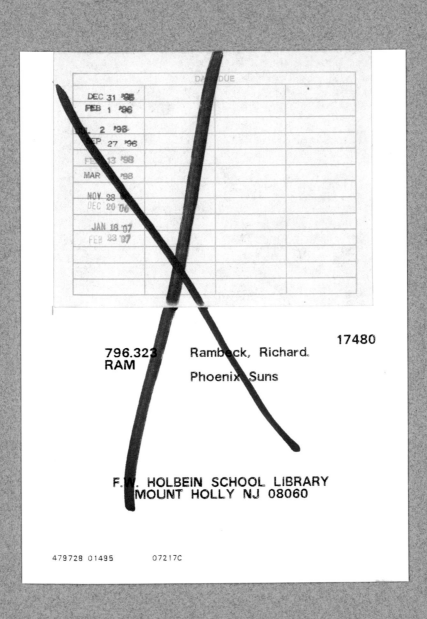

PHOENIX SUNS

RICHARD RAMBECK

COVER AND TITLE PAGE PHOTOS BY MATT MAHURIN

CREATIVE EDUCATION

Published by Creative Education, Inc.

123 S. Broad Street, Mankato, Minnesota 56001 USA

Art Director, Rita Marshall
Cover and title page photography by Matt Mahurin
Book design by Rita Marshall

Photos by: Allsport; Mel Bailey; Bettmann Archive;
Brian Drake; Duomo; Focus On Sports; FPG; South
Florida Images Inc.; Spectra-Action; Sportschrome;
Sports Photo Masters, Inc.; SportsLight: Brian Drake,
Long Photography; Wide World Photos.

Library of Congress Cataloging-in-Publication Data

Rambeck, Richard.

Phoenix Suns / Richard Rambeck.

Summary: A team history of the Phoenix Suns, the
first major-league professional sports team to be
headquartered in the state of Arizona.

ISBN 0-88682-520-2

1. Phoenix Suns (Basketball team)—History—
Juvenile literature. [1. Phoenix Suns (Basketball
team)—History. 2. Basketball—History.] I. Title.

GV885.52.P47R36 1992   92-3720

796.323'64'0979173—dc20   CIP

PHOENIX: HOME OF THE SUNS

The state of Arizona is known for its hot weather and its many breathtaking natural landmarks. Visitors are amazed by the beauty they encounter at places such as the Grand Canyon, Monument Valley, Oak Creek Canyon, and the Petrified Forest. These attractions and many others have made Arizona one of the nation's most popular vacation states.

Even with its dramatic scenery and excellent weather, Arizona's population grew slowly. Then, about 40 years ago, people from all parts of the United States "discovered" Arizona and began moving there. Many of them settled in Phoenix, the state capital, located in the south central part of Arizona. Phoenix grew incredibly fast. In 1950, it had only about 100,000 residents; now, with a population of nearly one million, Phoenix is one of the 10 largest cities in the United States.

In 1968, when officials of the National Basketball Association were thinking about expanding into new cities, they couldn't overlook the booming Phoenix area. On January 22, 1968, the NBA announced it was adding two new franchises to begin play in the fall of that year. One would be based in Milwaukee. The other would play in Phoenix, and would be the first major-league professional sports team to be headquartered in the state of Arizona.

The *Arizona Republic* sponsored a contest to name the team. More than 28,000 entries were submitted, ranging from "Gila Monsters" to "Roughriders." The winning entry was "Suns," which was a good choice because the area around Phoenix is known as the "Valley of the Sun."

1 9 6 9

Dick Van Arsdale represented the first-year Suns in the NBA All-Star Game.

THE HAWK SWOOPS INTO THE VALLEY

Phoenix's first pro franchise had a shining nickname, but it did not have shining success in its first season in the NBA. The Suns won only 16 games. That was the bad news. The good news was that Phoenix and Milwaukee would flip a coin to decide which team would have the first pick in the NBA draft. The prize in the draft was 7-foot-2 center Lew Alcindor, who would later change his name to Kareem Abdul-Jabbar. Alcindor had led UCLA to three straight NCAA basketball championships. Unfortunately, Phoenix general manager Jerry Colangelo lost the coin toss, and Alcindor went to Milwaukee. With their selection the Suns chose Neal Walk, a center from the University

Current Phoenix star Dan Majerle.

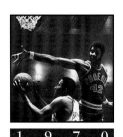

Connie Hawkins ranked sixth in the NBA in scoring and fourth in minutes played.

of Miami. Although Walk was a fine player, he was not nearly as talented as Alcindor.

The Suns lost out on one star during the college draft, but they didn't miss out on another great veteran player. His name was Connie Hawkins, and he had been a basketball legend for years. "The Hawk" had never performed in the NBA, however. Eight years earlier, Hawkins had been questioned by police about his possible involvement in a plot to fix college basketball games; although he was never found guilty of any crime, the NBA banned him from the league.

Hawkins, who was in college at the University of Iowa when the scandal occurred, suddenly couldn't compete either in college or in the NBA. He played for a while with the Harlem Globetrotters and then with the Pittsburgh Pipers in the American Basketball Association. Hawkins led the Pipers to the 1967-68 ABA championship and was named Most Valuable Player of the league.

But Hawkins, a long-armed 6-foot-8 forward, still wanted to play in the NBA. He and his lawyer filed a $6 million lawsuit against the NBA, claiming that the league had been unfair when it banned him. NBA officials told the Hawk that they would let him play in the league if he dropped his suit. Hawkins agreed, and the Suns were able to sign the star.

Led by Hawkins and forward Dick Van Arsdale, the Suns became the most improved team in the NBA during the 1969-70 season. They went from last place to the playoffs in just one year. Hawkins, who averaged 24.6 points a game, wound up starting for the Western Conference in the All-Star Game. Guard Gail Goodrich gave the Suns an outside shooting threat, and forward Paul Silas made the team even tougher inside. In the playoffs, the Suns took a three-games-to-one lead in the first-round series against the Los Angeles Lakers. The powerful Lakers then rallied to win three straight and claim the series.

Few teams in NBA history had become so good, so fast. Phoenix had made the playoffs in only its second season, and the main reason was Connie Hawkins. "Connie really took charge of some games like I've been waiting to see all year," said Colangelo, who took over as coach in the middle of the 1969-70 season. "He won some all by himself."

Opponents took note of the Hawk's many abilities. "Hawkins is a complete player," said New York Knicks coach Red Holzman. "You have to like him, because he plays both ends of the floor. I'd hate to see him get any better. He's too good now."

Paul Silas became the first Phoenix player to record 1,000 rebounds in a season.

COACHING CHANGES

Connie Hawkins may have been too good for some opponents, but his team still needed a lot of improvement to become a contender for an NBA title. Suns management took a risk by hiring Cotton Fitzsimmons, a small-college coach with no pro background, to lead the team. The gamble paid off as the new coach brought fresh ideas and enthusiasm to Phoenix and guided the team to two excellent seasons. Under Fitzsimmons, the Suns won 97 games and lost only 67 in the 1970-71 and 1971-72 seasons. But the team didn't make the playoffs either time. Fitzsimmons decided to resign before the 1972-73 season, and general manager Colangelo took over the coaching reins once again.

The following year, Colangelo left his position on the team bench and hired another college coach to lead the

Walter Davis' smooth play . . .

. . . reminded many of Connie Hawkins.

Charley Scott led the Suns in scoring with over 25 points per game.

Suns. His name was John MacLeod, and he had been very successful at the University of Oklahoma. Colangelo believed that MacLeod was the right person to take the Suns to a championship level. That belief, however, would be tested during MacLeod's first two years at the team's helm.

The Suns struggled, but it wasn't really the coach's fault. Key players such as Dick Van Arsdale and guard Charley Scott spent much of the time out of the lineup with injuries. In an attempt to turn things around, an aging Connie Hawkins was traded to the Los Angeles Lakers for forward Keith Erickson. But Erickson couldn't replace Hawkins because he, too, became injured. The Suns and MacLeod needed help. Luckily, it was on the way.

THE SUNS REVOLVE AROUND ADAMS

The Suns located the help they needed at the same college that had given them John MacLeod—the University of Oklahoma. Phoenix had the fourth pick in the 1975 NBA draft and used it to take 6-foot-9 center Alvan Adams, who had starred for the Sooners. MacLeod knew all about Adams, having coached him at Oklahoma when Adams was a freshman. During his college career, Adams was named Big Eight Conference Player of the Year after his freshman, sophomore, and junior seasons. He was also the Most Valuable Player of the Big Eight Tournament all three of those years. Adams might have earned even more honors, but he decided to leave school after his junior year. He was a good student, but he felt he had nothing left to prove as a basketball player at the college level.

Mike Bantom made over 500 rebounds and 150 assists throughout the season.

When Adams came to Phoenix, some of his teammates wondered if he was big enough and strong enough to play center in the NBA. One of those doubters was Phoenix guard Paul Westphal. But Westphal's opinion of Adams changed after the two played together in a summer league before the 1975-76 season. "I knew from that first game that he was good," Westphal explained. "Just by the way he handled himself, how he protected the ball, how he moved so smoothly." Adams stepped right into the Phoenix starting lineup, and the whole team began running very smoothly. The Suns loved the way Adams passed the ball, as well as how he rebounded and played defense. "Alvan surprised people his first time around," Colangelo recalled. "He's by far the best [draft] pick we've ever made. No question about

13

Rookie Alvan Adams topped Phoenix in rebounds, assists, and blocks and was second in points and steals.

it. He has great hands. He's an offensive threat passing the ball. It's nice to try to project what he'll be two or three years from now, with experience."

Even without much NBA experience, Adams played in the All-Star Game his rookie season. He also lifted the Suns to unexpected success. Although Phoenix was picked by many experts to be one of the worst teams in the league, the Suns made the playoffs, thanks to Adams, Westphal, and forwards Garfield Heard and Curtis Perry. Phoenix then defeated Seattle four games to two in a first-round playoff series. That earned the Suns the right to play defending NBA champion Golden State. No one gave Phoenix much of a chance against the Warriors, but the Suns won the series in seven games.

Phoenix faced off against the powerful Boston Celtics in the NBA championship series. Again the Suns were heavy underdogs. And again they gave the favored team an unexpected challenge. After splitting the first four games, the two teams played the fifth contest in Boston Garden. Many basketball experts consider that game to be the most exciting in NBA playoff history.

When regulation time expired, the Suns and Celtics were deadlocked at 95-95. Then, with just seconds left in the first overtime, Boston guard John Havlicek hit a clutch shot to tie the game once more. With two seconds left in the second overtime, Havlicek did it again—giving Boston a one-point lead.

That's when things got a little confusing. Boston added a free throw after Phoenix was given a technical foul for calling too many timeouts. Paul Westphal had suggested that the Suns take the "illegal" timeout so that they could get the ball at midcourt instead of under their own basket. Down

Sharpshooter Paul Westphal.

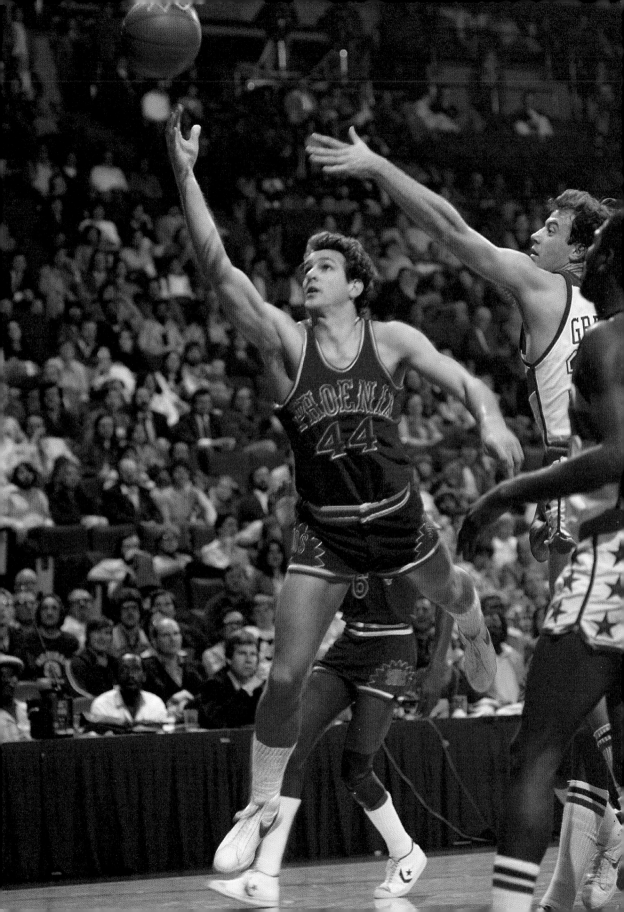

*Future Suns coach
Paul Westphal led the
Suns in scoring for
the second of five
consecutive seasons.*

by two with two seconds to go, Phoenix would have to
get off a fast accurate shot to tie the game. The inbounds
pass came to Garfield Heard 25 feet from the basket. Heard
was never known as a great outside shooter, particularly
from that distance. But he caught the ball, spun, and
launched one of the highest arching shots in league history.
Swish…tie game…a third overtime.

The Suns finally ran out of miracles in the third extra
period. Boston won the contest and then took game six in
Phoenix to win the series. The best season in the Suns' history had finally ended. The team, which had never even
won a playoff series before the 1975-76 season, had nearly
claimed the NBA championship. Alvan Adams was named
NBA Rookie of the Year. Jerry Colangelo was selected NBA
Executive of the Year. And most basketball fans in Phoenix
were convinced that John MacLeod could walk on water.

16

DAVIS BECOMES A SUNS STAR

Unfortunately for the Phoenix fans, the Suns couldn't duplicate the magic of the 1975-76 season. They struggled with injuries the following year. Only Paul Westphal, who was named to the All-NBA first team, was able to contribute full time.

Guard Don Buse was named to the NBA All-Defensive team for his outstanding play.

When the 1977-78 season started, the Suns had a new star in the frontcourt. He was a 6-foot-6 sharpshooter from the University of North Carolina. His name was Walter Davis, but he was also known as "Sweet D."

At North Carolina, Davis was a good player in a great system. Coach Dean Smith didn't believe in trying to create star players, only superb teams. Davis played well at North Carolina, but he didn't get noticed that much. "I felt like the kid who makes A's on his report card, but nobody said, 'Good work,'" Davis recalled. "Coach Smith kept me going, though."

Once Davis got to the NBA, he really got moving. He was almost unstoppable, in fact. In his rookie season, Davis played two games against the legendary Dr. J, Julius Erving. In those two games, Davis scored 64 points against Erving's defense. Curry Kirkpatrick, a writer for *Sports Illustrated*, noted that "against Sweet D, the good Doctor looked like a horse doctor."

Davis didn't believe that he had changed his game that much in going from North Carolina to Phoenix. "The only difference from last year is I'm wearing orange and white instead of blue and white," Davis said with a shrug.

Davis was named NBA Rookie of the Year after the 1977-78 season. The Suns made the playoffs that year, but lost in the first round to Milwaukee. The following season,

The Suns had an explosive attack (pages 18-19).

Truck Robinson averaged 11.6 rebounds per game, tops among NBA forwards.

Phoenix added power forward Leonard "Truck" Robinson in a trade with Utah. Robinson was a devastating rebounder and an excellent scorer. In fact, he was one of the toughest offensive rebounders in the league.

Unfortunately, Robinson came down with a virus during the season, but he was healthy in time for the playoffs. With Truck pounding the boards inside, Phoenix got past the first round of the 1979 playoffs by whipping the Portland Trail Blazers. Then Kansas City fell to the Suns, and Phoenix advanced to the Western Conference finals against the Seattle SuperSonics. Seattle won the first two games of the series, but the Suns came blazing back to claim the next three.

Phoenix had a chance to wrap up the series at home, but it was not to be. Ex-Sun Paul Silas inspired his Seattle teammates to a superior effort as the Sonics took the lead in the fourth quarter. With time running out and the Suns trailing by a basket, Phoenix got the ball to Garfield Heard. Three years earlier, Heard had buried a clutch jumper in overtime against Boston in the NBA finals. This time, his shot bounced off the rim, and Paul Silas cradled the rebound. Seattle went on to win the game by a single point, and then captured the series a few nights later.

Phoenix players were tremendously disappointed. Unfortunately, their luck in the playoffs didn't improve in subsequent seasons, despite having one of the best teams in the league. For example, in 1980-81, Phoenix won its first-ever division title, but the Suns flamed out against Kansas City in the second round of the playoffs. Two years later, the Suns, who had won more than 50 games during the regular season, were expected to burn past the Denver Rockets in the first round of the playoffs. Once again, Phoenix faltered.

Despite the Suns' playoff misfortunes, MacLeod decided not to change the foundation of the team, which was built around Alvan Adams and Walter Davis. But the Phoenix coach did try to strengthen the structure by trading Westphal to Seattle for guard Dennis Johnson. Johnson had good years in Phoenix, but he couldn't help lead the team to a championship. More changes were needed.

First, Dennis Johnson was traded to Boston for center Rick Robey. Then Walter Davis, who had been a forward on the team, was moved to guard to allow 6-foot-10 Larry Nance to join the starting lineup. In addition, Truck Robinson was traded to New York for veteran power forward Maurice Lucas. By the time the 1983-84 season began, the Suns believed they had created a championship team. They were almost right.

John MacLeod directed the West team in the NBA All-Star Game, the only Suns coach to earn that honor.

Power forward Maurice Lucas.

The Suns posted only a 41-41 record during the regular season, but they caught fire in the playoffs. Phoenix beat Portland in the first round and Midwest Division champion Utah in the second round. For the first time in four years, the Suns were in the Western Conference finals. Their opponent was the Los Angeles Lakers, who had won the last two conference crowns. The Lakers managed to make it three straight, but the determined Suns put up a hard fight in a six-game battle.

Phoenix fans, based on their club's fine performance in the 1984 playoffs, were optimistic that the franchise's first NBA championship trophy would soon be on display in the Valley of the Sun. But their hopes fell quickly as the Suns got off to a slow start in 1984-85. Those hopes really collapsed when, a quarter of the way through the year, Walter Davis announced that he was leaving the club to enter a drug rehabilitation program. There were rumors that Davis wasn't the only Sun with such a problem. Those rumors haunted the club for two seasons, and the Suns' performance suffered. The team recorded its first losing seasons in nearly a decade. Midway through the second year, John MacLeod was fired, and former Phoenix star Dick Van Arsdale completed the 1986-87 season at the Suns' helm. The next year, John Wetzel took over, but he, too, was soon gone; under Wetzel, the Suns managed only 28 victories, the lowest total in the club's 20-year history.

That was the bad news. But, luckily for Phoenix fans, there was good news as well. During the dismal 1987-88 season, the Suns traded forwards Larry Nance and Mike Sanders to the Cleveland Cavaliers for center Mark West and a young point guard named Kevin Johnson. Phoenix

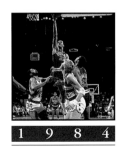

1 9 8 4

High-flying forward Larry Nance won the first All-Star weekend slam-dunk contest.

Left to right: Eddie Johnson, Jeff Hornacek, Armon Gilliam, Mark West.

gave up a lot in the trade—Larry Nance had already established himself as an NBA star—but the Suns may have gotten even more in return.

KJ PUTS SUNSHINE BACK IN THE PHOENIX OFFENSE

The key to the Suns' trade with the Cavaliers was Kevin Johnson, and he turned out to be just what the club needed to pep up its halting attack. Almost instantly, KJ established himself as one of the top point guards in the NBA. Amazingly, Cleveland had been willing to trade the young speedster because Johnson hadn't been able to crack their starting lineup.

Walter Davis led Phoenix in scoring for the fourth time in five years.

Johnson had been selected by Cleveland with the seventh pick in the 1987 NBA draft. The Cavaliers took him even though they already had a good young point guard, Mark Price. "I figured they were grooming him to put me on the bench," Price recalled. But Price was the one who won "the battle of the point" in Cleveland. "He outplayed me so badly there was no doubt he was better," Johnson said of Price.

Johnson didn't get much chance to play in Cleveland, but he moved right into the Phoenix starting lineup. He teamed with forwards Armond Gilliam and Eddie Johnson to give the Suns a solid offense. That offense soon got a lot more firepower when Tom Chambers was signed as a free agent before the 1988-89 season.

Chambers, one of the most explosive scorers in the league, averaged 25.7 points a game during his first year in Phoenix. His scoring touch seemed to be contagious. Forward Eddie Johnson tossed in more than 21 points a game,

Kevin Johnson (pages 26-27).

After arriving in Phoenix in midseason, Kevin Johnson averaged nearly nine assists and 13 points per game.

and Kevin Johnson added more than 20 per contest. In addition, reserve forward Dan Majerle showed he was an outstanding defender and an underrated scorer, and sharp-shooting guard Jeff Hornacek proved to be an ideal backcourt mate to Kevin Johnson.

All of the players contributed, but KJ was the key man as Phoenix rolled to a 55-27 record in 1988-89—an amazing 27-victory improvement over the previous season. The Suns' record earned them second place in the Pacific Division behind the Los Angeles Lakers.

Johnson brought both speed and finesse to the Suns' attack. He was lightning quick on the court and could beat opponents with either his shooting or his passing. During the 1988-89 season, KJ averaged 20.4 points and 12.2 assists per game. "Every time he gets the ball," explained former Chicago coach Doug Collins, "he has a chance to break your defense."

Phoenix coach Cotton Fitzsimmons, who had been rehired before the 1988-89 season, could only smile at his good fortune to have KJ running his club's offense. "Nobody in the NBA can guard this kid," said Fitzsimmons.

With Johnson leading the attack, the Suns advanced all the way to the Western Conference finals in 1988-89, where they were swept in four games by the Lakers. But the team was not discouraged. The following season, Phoenix had another outstanding campaign and reached the conference finals for the second straight year. This time, the Suns faced off against the Portland Trail Blazers. The playoff series turned out to be both exciting and frustrating for Phoenix players and fans.

In game one, Phoenix trailed Portland, 100-98, with only five seconds left in the contest. Suns reserve guard

Tom Chambers'
2,085 points scored
and 25.7 average set
all-time Suns records.

Mike McGee had an open shot from the right corner that could tie the game. But out of nowhere came Portland guard Danny Young, who blocked McGee's shot and assured the Blazers' win.

In game two, Phoenix raced to an 18-point halftime lead. In the second half the Blazers roared back and, with just 12 seconds left, they went ahead, 108-107. KJ then rushed the ball upcourt to Eddie Johnson (EJ), who had an open jumper from almost the same spot that McGee had had at the end of game one. The result was almost the same. Portland's Jerome Kersey leaped at EJ and forced him to rush his shot. The ball fell short, and the Suns had another close loss.

Phoenix bounced back to tie the series with two victories at home. But the Blazers were not to be denied, and they eliminated the Suns from the playoffs in six games.

The powerful X-Man: Xavier McDaniel.

High-scoring forward Tom Chambers. 31

LOOKING FORWARD TO A SUNNY FUTURE

The Suns acquired superstar Charles Barkley in a trade with Philadelphia.

The Suns rebounded from their heartbreaking setback at the Blazers' hands to post another fine year in 1990-91. During the season Phoenix traded Eddie Johnson, who was unhappy about his lack of playing time, to Seattle for forward Xavier McDaniel. Known as the X-Man, McDaniel was a former All-Star who was a solid scorer and rebounder. Despite the addition of McDaniel and the continued improved play of Dan Majerle, the Suns were beaten in the first round of the 1991 playoffs by the Utah Jazz. Before the next season, McDaniel was gone in a trade with the New York Knicks for young forward/center Jarrod Mustaf. Suns coach Fitzsimmons decided that the X-Man was expendable because of the presence of two young forwards on the team—Cedric Ceballos and Tim Perry—who had earned the right to more playing time.

Since the arrival of Kevin Johnson in Phoenix during the 1986-87 season, the Suns have been almost totally revamped and their fortunes have been turned around. The addition of players such as Tom Chambers, Dan Majerle, Jeff Hornacek, and Mark West has made the Suns one of the hottest offensive powers in the West. With the added presence of young future stars such as Ceballos, Perry, and Mustaf, the Suns figure to be among the best teams in the NBA for years to come. It may not be long before the team from the Valley of the Sun reaches the top of the NBA mountain.